W9-ACX-771

WITHDRAWN

06/15

PRAIRIE DU CHIEN MEMORIAL LIBRARY

125 S. Wacouta Ave.

Prairie du Chien, WI 53821

(608) 326-6211

Mon/Thur 9-8   Fri 9-5   Sat 9-1

WITHDRAWN

Exploring Food Chains and Food Webs

MEADOW
FOOD CHAINS

Katie Kawa

PowerKiDS
press.

New York

Prairie du Chien
Memorial Library
125 Wacouta Ave.
Prairie du Chien WI 53821

18.00 06/15

Published in 2015 by The Rosen Publishing Group, Inc.
29 East 21st Street, New York, NY 10010

Copyright © 2015 by The Rosen Publishing Group, Inc.

All rights reserved. No part of this book may be reproduced in any form without permission in writing from the publisher, except by a reviewer.

First Edition

Editor: Katie Kawa
Book Design: Reann Nye

Photo Credits: Cover chillchill_lanla/Shutterstock.com; pp. 5, 21 (dandelion) Martin Ruegner/Photolibrary/Getty Images; pp. 5, 21 (grasshopper) QiuJu Song/Shutterstock.com; pp. 5, 21 (praying mantis) Czesznak Zsolt/Shutterstock.com; p. 5 (background) Roxana Bashyrova/Shutterstock.com; p. 7 Michael Wheatley/All Canada Photos/Getty Images; p. 9 djgis/Shutterstock.com; p. 10 Darlyne A. Murawski/National Geographic/Getty Images; p. 11 Don Mammoser/Shutterstock.com; p. 12 Pictureguy/Shutterstock.com; pp. 13, 21 (vole) Matthieu Berroneau/Moment Open/Getty Images; pp. 14, 21 (red-tailed hawk) Tony Moran/Shutterstock.com; p. 15 Stephen Mcsweeny/Shutterstock.com; p. 17 Kaido KArner/E+/Getty Images; pp. 18, 21 (earthworm) Ed Reschke/Stockbyte/Getty Images; pp. 19, 21 (mushroom) Johannes Dag Mayer/Shutterstock.com; p. 21 (red fox) Soru Epotok/Shutterstock.com; p. 21 (grass) Smileus/Shutterstock.com; p. 21 (owl) Leena Robinson/Shutterstock.com; p. 21 (deer) Tom Reichner/Shutterstock.com; p. 21 (wildflowers) Edmund Lowe Photography/Shutterstock.com; p. 21 (hummingbird) TMore Campbell/Shutterstock.com; p. 21 (background) Nadia Borisevich/Shutterstock.com; p. 22 Nemeziya/Shutterstock.com.

Library of Congress Cataloging-in-Publication Data

Kawa, Katie.
Meadow food chains / by Katie Kawa.
p. cm. — (Exploring food chains and food webs)
Includes index.
ISBN 978-1-4994-0157-8 (pbk.)
ISBN 978-1-4994-0159-2 (6-pack)
ISBN 978-1-4994-0155-4 (library binding)
1. Meadow ecology — Juvenile literature. 2. Food chains (Ecology) — Juvenile literature. I. Kawa, Katie. II. Title.
QH541.5.M4 K39 2015
577.4—d23

Manufactured in the United States of America

CPSIA Compliance Information: Batch #CW15PK: For Further Information contact Rosen Publishing, New York, New York at 1-800-237-9932

CONTENTS

MAKING MEADOW FOOD CHAINS

A meadow is a common place to see food chains in action. What's a food chain? It's a way of showing how the living things in a **habitat** are connected by the flow of **energy**. All living things need energy, and they get it from food. Each time energy is passed on by one living thing eating another, a **link** is added to the food chain.

A food web shows the way many food chains come together in one habitat, such as a meadow. Every living thing in a meadow is part of a food chain.

Food Chain Fact

Dandelions are common meadow plants. They get their energy from the sun.

GRASSHOPPER

DANDELION

PRAYING MANTIS

This food chain shows how energy is passed from one living thing to another in a meadow. A grasshopper gets energy from eating a dandelion, and a praying mantis gets energy from eating a grasshopper.

SHORT AND TALL GRASSES

If you ever visit a meadow, the first things you'll notice are grasses. A meadow is an open field that's covered with different kinds of grasses. Some grasses are short, but others are taller than a person! There aren't many trees in a meadow habitat.

Some meadows are found in the mountains, but many are found where the land is flat. Meadow grasses sometimes grow in areas where farmers once cleared the land for crops. These grasses provide food and homes for many animals.

Food Chain Fact

Meadows commonly get a lot of sunlight because there are few trees to block the sun.

Colorful wildflowers often grow alongside the grasses in a meadow habitat.

STARTING WITH THE SUN

All the plants in a meadow need the sun for energy. They use the energy from the sun to make, or produce, their own food. This is why plants are also called producers. Plants are the first link in a meadow food chain.

Plants use energy from the sun to turn water and a gas in the air called carbon dioxide into a kind of sugar. This **process** is called photosynthesis (foh-toh-SIHN-thuh-suhs). Plants also produce oxygen during photosynthesis, which is a gas animals need to live.

Food Chain Fact

When animals eat plants, some of the sun's energy is passed on to them.

The sun is helping these meadow plants make their own food.

WHAT'S POLLINATION?

The wildflowers in a meadow **attract** birds and **insects** with their bright colors. These birds and insects drink the nectar from these flowers for food. In return, they help flowers reproduce, or make new flowers.

Birds and insects carry pollen from one flower to another. Pollen needs to reach another flower of the same species, or kind, to make new flowers. This process is called pollination. Flowers need birds and insects to reproduce. Birds and insects need flowers for food. They help each other get what they need.

Food Chain Fact

Nectar is a sweet juice found in flowers.

Hummingbirds eat insects and nectar, and they help spread pollen to make new flowers in a meadow.

11

THE SECOND LINK

A meadow habitat is filled with hungry herbivores. These are animals that eat only plants. Herbivores are the second link in a meadow food chain. The white-tailed deer is a common meadow herbivore. It eats the grasses in a meadow and uses them to hide from predators.

A meadow vole is another herbivore. It's also known as a meadow mouse. A meadow vole eats grasses and seeds. In the winter, it might also eat the roots of some plants. Meadow voles are known for having many babies.

White-tailed deer and meadow voles are important parts of food chains. They eat plants, and then other animals eat them.

Food Chain Fact

A mother meadow vole can have over 50 babies in one year.

13

BIRDS THAT HUNT

Animals can often be seen running across or flying over a meadow as they hunt their **prey**. Animals that eat other animals are called carnivores, and they make up another link in a meadow food chain.

Red-tailed hawks hunt meadow voles and other small **rodents**. Red-tailed hawks are then hunted by great horned owls. Great horned owls eat many other animals in a meadow, including voles and rabbits. They grab prey in their large talons, or claws, and sometimes swallow it whole. Great horned owls are nocturnal, which means they're most active at night.

Great horned owls don't often eat adult red-tailed hawks. They hunt these birds when they're babies.

RED-TAILED HAWK

15

Food Chain Fact

Great horned owls eat other carnivores, such as the red-tailed hawk. Carnivores that eat other carnivores are called secondary carnivores.

OMNIVORES AREN'T PICKY

Some animals in a meadow aren't picky when it comes to eating. They'll eat both plants and animals. These animals are known as omnivores. People are a good example of omnivores. Red foxes are omnivores that eat voles, rabbits, and fruit. They've also been known to eat out of garbage cans.

Red foxes eat the bodies of dead animals, too. Animals that do this are called scavengers. They're an important part of all food chains. Scavengers make sure the energy stored in a dead animal's body doesn't go to waste.

Food Chain Fact

Red foxes often store food to eat at a later time. They put the food in a hole in the ground and cover it with dirt. This is called caching.

Red foxes are found in habitats all over the world, including meadows, deserts, forests, and even neighborhoods where people live.

LIFE IN THE SOIL

When meadow plants and animals die, their bodies are broken down in the soil. The living things that break them down are called decomposers. When decomposers break down dead plants and animals, they put **nutrients** back into the soil. These nutrients help new plants grow, which starts a new food chain.

Earthworms are meadow decomposers that live in the soil. Other decomposers include bacteria and **fungi**. Mushrooms are fungi often seen in a meadow. They grow above the ground and have a stem and cap.

Food Chain Fact

Some decomposers are food for other animals. For example, people eat certain kinds of mushrooms.

These decomposers help keep the soil in a meadow healthy so new plants can grow.

A MEADOW FOOD WEB

The plants and animals in a meadow depend on each other for energy. This food web shows the connections between the living things in several meadow food chains. The arrows show the flow of energy from one living thing to another. The colors used on the food web highlight the different kinds of living things found in a meadow. The decomposers, which are shown in gray on the food web, break down every living thing in this web after it dies.

Food Web Key

- carnivore
- decomposer
- herbivore
- omnivore
- producer

Food Chain Fact

A praying mantis can catch and eat a hummingbird.

WHITE-TAILED DEER

MUSHROOM

EARTHWORM

GRASS

DANDELION

WILDFLOWERS

MEADOW VOLE

GRASSHOPPER

HUMMINGBIRD

RED FOX

PRAYING MANTIS

RED-TAILED HAWK

GREAT HORNED OWL

A CHANGING HABITAT

A meadow is a good place to study many things about the natural world, including food chains and food webs. Some people live near meadows, which makes it easy for them to study the living things in this habitat and the connections between them.

A meadow habitat changes with the seasons. It's not the same in the hot summer as it is in the cold winter. It's fun to visit a meadow and see the **variety** of living things that call this habitat home.

Food Chain Fact

Meadows don't get as much sunlight in the winter as they do in the summer. This affects the growth of meadow plants.

GLOSSARY

attract: To cause to come close.

energy: The power or ability to be active.

fungi: Living things, such as mushrooms and mold, that feed on dead plants and animals.

habitat: The natural home for plants, animals, and other living things.

insect: A small animal with a body divided into three parts, three pairs of jointed legs, and commonly one or two pairs of wings.

link: A connecting piece.

nutrient: Something taken in by a plant or animal that helps it grow and stay healthy.

prey: An animal hunted by other animals for food.

process: A series of actions or changes.

rodent: Any small mammal that has sharp front teeth that are always growing and are used for biting and chewing.

variety: A number or collection of different things.

INDEX

WEBSITES

Due to the changing nature of Internet links, PowerKids Press has developed an online list of websites related to the subject of this book. This site is updated regularly. Please use this link to access the list: www.powerkidslinks.com/fcfw/mfc